NEW VANGUARD • 153

M551 SHERIDAN

US Airmobile Tanks 1941–2001

STEVEN J ZALOGA　　　ILLUSTRATED BY TONY BRYAN

First published in Great Britain in 2009 by Osprey Publishing,
Midland House, West Way, Botley, Oxford, OX2 0PH, UK
443 Park Avenue South, New York, NY 10016, USA
E-mail: info@ospreypublishing.com

A CIP catalog record for this book is available from the British Library

Print ISBN: 978 1 84603 391 9
PDF e-book ISBN: 978 1 84603 873 0

Page layout by: Melissa Orrom Swan, Oxford
Index by Peter Finn
Typeset in Sabon and Myriad Pro
Originated by PDQ Digital Media Solutions
Printed in China through Worldprint Ltd.

09 10 11 12 13   10 9 8 7 6 5 4 3 2 1

FOR A CATALOG OF ALL BOOKS PUBLISHED BY OSPREY MILITARY AND
AVIATION PLEASE CONTACT:

NORTH AMERICA

Osprey Direct, c/o Random House Distribution Center, 400 Hahn Road,
Westminster, MD 21157
E-mail: uscustomerservice@ospreypublishing.com

ALL OTHER REGIONS

Osprey Direct, The Book Service Ltd, Distribution Centre, Colchester Road,
Frating Green, Colchester, Essex, CO7 7DW, UK
E-mail: customerservice@ospreypublishing.com

Osprey Publishing is supporting the Woodland Trust, the UK's leading
woodland conservation charity, by funding the dedication of trees.

www.ospreypublishing.com

AUTHOR'S NOTE

The author would especially like to thank Colonel Russ Vaughan (USAR –
Ret'd) for his help with the photos for this book and for sharing his
recollections of the Sheridan from his service with the 2nd Armored Cavalry
and 82nd Airborne divisions.

GLOSSARY

ACAV	armored cavalry vehicle
ACR	Armored Cavalry Regiment
AFV	armored fighting vehicle
AGS	Armored Gun System
AMC	Army Materiel Command
APC	armored personnel carrier
APG	Aberdeen Proving Ground
ARAAV	Armored Reconnaissance Airborne Assault Vehicle
CBSS	closed breech scavenging system
CCVL	Close Combat Vehicle – Light
CVWS	Combat Vehicle Weapon System
DARPA	Defense Advanced Research Programs Agency
ELKE	Elevated Kinetic Energy
FY	Fiscal Year
HEAT	high-explosive antitank
HEAT-T-MP	high-explosive antitank-tracer-multi-purpose
HE-Frag	high-explosive/fragmentation
HSTV-L	High Survivability Test Vehicle – Light
LAPES	low-altitude parachute extraction system
LVAD	low-velocity air drop
MACV	Military Assistance Command, Vietnam
MBT	main battle tank
MERADCOM	Mobility Equipment Research And Development Command
MERDC	Mobility Equipment Research and Development Center
NBC	nuclear, biological, chemical
OBSS	open breech scavenging system
OTAC	Ordnance Tank Automotive Command
PDF	Panamanian Defense Forces
SACLOS	semi-automatic command line-of-sight
SPAT	Self-Propelled Anti-Tank (the M56 90mm Scorpion SPAT)
TACOM	Tank and Automotive Command
TECOM	Test and Evaluation Command
TOW	Tube-Launched, Optically Tracked, Wire-Guided missile
TRADOC	Training and Doctrine Command
TTS	Tank Thermal Sight
USAAF	US Army Air Forces
USAREUR	US Army Europe
USMC	United States Marine Corps
VISMOD	Visual Modification vehicles
WSMR	White Sands Missile Range

CONTENTS

M551 SHERIDAN
US AIRBORNE TANKS: 1941–2001

INTRODUCTION

The birth of airborne forces in World War II led to the first serious attempts to develop light tanks suitable for air-delivery to provide offensive support for paratroopers. The US Army developed its first airborne tanks during the war, but the lack of convenient means of delivery severely limited their employment. With the advent of more substantial transport aircraft during the Cold War, however, further efforts were made to develop airborne armored vehicles. The most ambitious of these programs was the M551 Sheridan, which incorporated a variety of new technologies, including futuristic hybrid gun/missile armament. It was the most powerful light tank ever fielded, but it had a trouble-plagued career due to its over-ambitious armament.

The Sheridan was first deployed as an armored cavalry vehicle in Vietnam, where its light armor and technological immaturity undermined its combat effectiveness. Although widely utilized in the armored cavalry role in Europe in the 1970s, its recurring technical problems led to its hasty retirement hardly a decade after its introduction. It remained in service with a single airborne armor battalion of the 82nd Airborne Division, and was the first tank ever parachuted into combat, during Operation *Just Cause* in Panama in 1989. It saw combat again in Iraq in 1991 during Operation *Desert Storm*, the only occasion where its Shillelagh guided missile was fired in anger. Eventually shorn of its powerful but troublesome armament, the Sheridan was widely used in the training role at the National Training Center in the Mojave desert before its final retirement in 2004. There were several attempts to replace it, including the little known M8 Armored Gun System, but to date the Sheridan remains the last US airborne tank.

AIRBORNE ARMOR

The US Army considered forming special airborne tank units after the successful use of German paratroopers at Eben Emael in 1940 and on Crete in 1941. The US Army Air Forces (USAAF), the Armored Force, and the Ordnance Department had first discussed the technical requirements for an airborne tank in February 1941, and the program was formally initiated in May 1941 as the T9 aero tank. There was no serious consideration given to parachuting the tank, as suitable large parachutes did not exist at the time. Instead, the initial scheme was to carry the tank under a transport aircraft and air-land it once a suitable airfield had been captured by paratroopers or

The M551A1(TTS) was the final variant of the Sheridan in service and one is seen here during training with 3/73rd Armor at Ft Bragg in 1991, still in its Operation *Desert Storm* colors. (Author)

glider infantry. British officials expressed interest in the program, which could support their own airborne divisions.

The eccentric designer J. Walter Christie had proposed flying tank designs on numerous occasions, including a glider with the tank serving as the fuselage, and a more conventional design that could be carried under a bomber. Christie was asked to bid on the program and offered a design in the autumn of 1941. The first design did not meet the size requirements, nor did a revised design in November 1941, so Christie was subsequently ignored. The Marmon-Herrington Company proposed its own design in July 1941, and work on a wooden mock-up and pilot vehicle was approved on August 31, 1941. Marmon-Herrington had already built light tanks for the US Marine Corps (USMC) and commercial export tanks for the Netherlands East Indies. The T9 was designed to be air-landed using the new Douglas C-54 transport aircraft, the military version of the DC-4 airliner. The tank hull would be suspended under the aircraft with the turret and crew carried inside. The Pontiac Division of General Motors also proposed a version using Pontiac engines instead of the Lycoming aircraft engine selected by Marmon-Herrington, but this was not pursued due to its high cost. A wooden mock-up of the hull was completed in November 1941 to test the interface between the tank and C-54 transport, and the pilot T9 was completed in April 1942 and set to Ft Benning for testing. Between the initial design and the pilot, the

The Marmon Herrington M22 aero light tank was the first US Army tank developed specifically for airborne use. (Patton Museum)

weight of the tank had crept over the 7.9-ton limit, and a redesign followed that eliminated some features such as the gun stabilizer, turret power traverse, and fixed bow machine guns to save weight. At the end of 1941, the Army planned to acquire about 500 T9 tanks for airborne operations. Marmon-Herrington also proposed a soft-steel, turretless version for use by the field artillery to tow the new M2 105mm howitzer. Although the artillery showed no interest, the Airborne Command sponsored the construction of a single T18 Cargo Carrier (Airborne), which could be used to tow the smaller M3 105mm howitzer. This vehicle was not accepted for production.

Based on the early trials, the design was substantially modified into a more suitable production configuration as the T9E1, with a wooden mockup completed in April 1942, and two pilot tanks in November 1942. One of the T9E1 pilots was sent to Britain and in April 1943 the accompanying team reported back that it had been well received and that the British preferred the design to their own Tetrarch airborne tank. The team also reported that Britain wanted to obtain T9E1 tanks at "an early date" and that they planned to deliver them into combat using a heretofore secret heavy glider, the Hamilcar. Production was scheduled to begin in November 1942, but was delayed until April 1943 due to lingering technical problems.

Although the Ordnance Department had been generally pleased with the T9E1, the Armored Board at Ft Knox offered a startlingly different opinion after its own tests. Its September 1943 preliminary report concluded that the "Light Tank T9E1 is not a satisfactory combat vehicle in its present state of development due to the lack of adequate reliability and durability … and cannot be used for landing operations with any degree of success." The Armored Board was particularly unhappy with the transmission, and recommended a variety of improvements to the powertrain and turret. The Board was so unhappy with the design that following the release of its final report on January 31, 1944, the Army decided to limit production in 1944 to the remaining 150 tanks from the March 1943 contract and terminate any

further production. Although there were plans to acquire as many as 1,900 T9E1s, in the event only 830 tanks were built. Due to the dissatisfaction with the design, the T9E1 was not formally approved until October 5, 1944, as the M22 light tank, and classified only as "limited standard."

In August 1942, the US Army formed its first two airborne divisions, built around experimental paratroop and glider infantry regiments. With development of the T9 aero tank underway, in February 1943 the Army Ground Forces ordered the Armored Force to organize an airborne tank battalion and develop suitable training and doctrine in cooperation with the Airborne Command. However, the Airborne Command was skeptical about the need for a battalion-sized formation due to the airlift problem posed by such a large organization, so the first unit was trimmed down to a company. The 151st Airborne Tank Company was activated at Ft Knox on August 15,

Derivatives of the M22 aero light tank included the T18 tractor, intended to tow airborne artillery. It never entered serial production. (NARA)

The 28th Tank Battalion at Ft Knox was the only US battalion entirely equipped with the M22, but it was formed too late to take part in the Normandy landings. (Patton Museum)

The advent of heavy-lift transports such as the Fairchild C-82 Packet after World War II made air-landing the M22 aero light tank more viable, but interest waned due to its meager firepower.

1943. In spite of the concerns about the amount of transport capacity that would be available, the 28th Airborne Tank Battalion was organized, starting on December 6, 1943.

The Airborne Command had no practical way to deliver the T9E1 into combat. The USAAF acquired a single British Hamilcar glider for trials, but no effort was made during the war to develop a comparable heavy-lift glider. The method of air-landing the T9E1 with the C-54 was inordinately cumbersome, and in the event the US airborne divisions conducted no air-landing operations during the war, only paratroop and glider landings. The USAAF began the development of a more satisfactory heavy transport in 1942, the Fairchild C-82 Packet, which had the capacity to carry the T9E1 intact within its fuselage and unload it through rear clamshell doors. This aircraft, however, did not enter production until September 1945.

The 151st Airborne Tank Company was not available in time for deployment with airborne units on D-Day, and in July 1944 was transferred from Ft Knox to Camp Mackall, North Carolina, where it was quickly forgotten. Due to the lack of interest by Airborne Command, the 28th Airborne Tank Battalion was reorganized as a conventional tank battalion in October 1944. A total of 25 M22 tanks were ordered for the European Theater of Operations (ETO) in April 1944 and delivered in September 1944. A small number were sent to the Sixth Army Group in Alsace in 1944 for

 M22 AERO LIGHT TANK, CO. B, 28TH TANK BATTALION, FT KNOX, 1944
The M22 was finished in the standard US Army lusterless olive drab. For reasons that are unclear, the 28th Battalion painted an unusually large number of stars on the sides of their tanks, including two on the turret. The individual vehicle name "Bonnie" follows the usual pattern, beginning with the company letter "B."

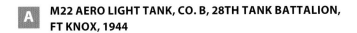

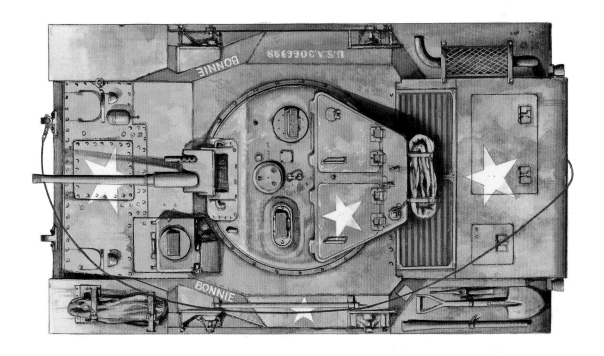

The M56 90mm Scorpion SPAT (Self-Propelled Anti-Tank) was Airborne Command's only tracked fighting vehicle in the late 1950s and early 1960s. As can be seen, the gun was mounted on a traversing, open pedestal, and the crew was entirely exposed. (Patton Museum)

potential use by the 1st Airborne Task Force. The fate of the M22s sent to the ETO, however, remains a mystery and there is little evidence that they saw combat in the hands of US troops.

Of the 830 M22 aero light tanks manufactured, 230 were supplied to Britain under Lend-Lease, where they were called the Locust. A T9E1 pilot was sent to Britain and first flew in a Hamilcar glider on July 13, 1943, to demonstrate the fit. Further evaluation by the Armoured Fighting Vehicle (AFV) School at Lulworth concluded that "this vehicle has shown itself to have a number of weak points both from a mechanical and gunnery point of view … it is just adequate for its intended role." The first 17 production T9E1s were issued to the British 6th Airborne Armoured Reconnaissance Regiment (AARR) in October 1943 to supplement its existing Tetrarch light tanks. Local modifications included the addition of smoke-mortars and modest stowage changes. Some tanks were also fitted with the Littlejohn Adapter, a barrel extension to increase the muzzle velocity of the 37mm gun and so improve its anti-armor capability. Although the original plans for D-Day envisioned the delivery of 17 Locusts and three Tetrarchs with 3in howitzers by Hamicar glider, the Locusts were temporarily removed from service due to technical concerns about various elements, including the transmission. The improved tanks manufactured during January 1944 dealt with this problem, but they did not arrive in time to be used in Normandy.

By the time of Operation *Varsity*, the airborne landings over the Rhine in March 1945, two Locust troops of the 6th AARR were allotted to the plan, with a total of eight tanks. During the air assault mission on March 24, 1945, one of the Hamilcars was lost during the approach when the Locust became loose inside and crashed through the rear of the glider. The remaining seven Hamilcars with their Locusts landed, but one Hamilcar lost a portion of its wing, hit a ditch and spilled out the tank at high speed – the tank somersaulted and landed on its roof. Of the remaining six Locusts, one went into support of US paratroopers of the 513th Parachute Infantry,

17th Airborne Division, and was knocked out by a German self-propelled gun, most likely a StuG III of Sturmgeschütz Brigade 394. Another suffered a mechanical breakdown while towing a jeep out of a Horsa glider, but remained in action during the day supporting the 12th Parachute Battalion. Only half of the Locusts actually managed to reach the rendezvous point and of these, one had a damaged 37mm gun and the other a damaged radio. The Locusts saw combat during the first day in support of the divisional HQ, but their value was undermined by the modest firepower offered by the 37mm gun, especially its small high-explosive round. The *Varsity* deployment was the only significant combat use of the M22 light aero tank in World War II. The US Army had recognized the shortcomings of the 37mm gun and began

The 1950s saw considerable experimentation with air-mobile tactics using helicopters. Here, a M56 SPAT re-armed with a lighter 106mm recoilless rifle is airlifted using one of the massive H-37 Mojave helicopters at Ft Benning in August 1958. (NARA)

This shows an M56 packed on its expendable parachute platform at the Yuma Test Station in January 1962. (NARA)

development of the 75mm T24E1 breech-loaded mortar as a possible substitute on the proposed T9E2 light aero tank. The program was not completed before the end of the war, however, and was abandoned.

Curiously enough, a handful of Locusts saw combat three years later in the 1948 Arab-Israeli War in Palestine. Britain provided Egypt with a small number of surplus Locusts after the war, and some were used by the Egyptian Army in the 1948 war against Israeli combat units.

COLD WAR AIRBORNE TANKS

The advent of the Fairchild C-82 Packet offered some hope for a viable airborne tank capability for US airborne divisions. The C-82 could carry and unload a combat-ready M22 tank. However, the British experience with the Locust had made it clear that its armament was not sufficient for the modern battlefield and the M22 was retired from US Army service after the war. Experiments were conducted on the delivery of the M24 light tank by air, but this tank was too heavy for the C-82 and could only be delivered in pieces by removing the turret and carrying this as a separate load. It took hours to re-build the M24 after unloading it from a pair of C-82s and this was too cumbersome a process to be practical. The advent of the much superior Fairchild C-119 Boxcar and C-123 Globemaster offered greater airlift capacity, but the US Army showed little interest in a dedicated airborne tank design through the mid-1950s. US light tank development work for the

The M56 Scorpion saw combat service with Co. D, 16th Armor of the 173rd Airborne Brigade in Vietnam, but the exposed crew position rendered it vulnerable to enemy small-arms fire. (US Army)

LOCUST, 6TH AIRBORNE ARMOURED RECONNAISSANCE REGIMENT, OPERATION *VARSITY*, MARCH 1945

British Locusts were finished in US lusterless olive drab or its British equivalent, SCC.15. There is a bit of a mystery whether the 6th AARR vehicles carried the full array of training markings as seen here, or whether they were painted over for the operation; clear photos are scarce. In the event, the usual markings on the bow consisted of the arm-of-service – white 41 on a green/blue square – a bridge weight symbol consisting of a black seven on a yellow circle, and the divisional insignia. The tactical symbol was painted on the turret and the census number on the hull side. A Hamilcar glider is evident in the background.

decade from 1945 to 1955 was concentrated on light tanks used in the armored cavalry role. The M41 Walker Bulldog light tank was manufactured to replace the wartime M24 light tank and the futuristic T92 light tank was tested as a possible replacement for the M41. There was some consideration of the T92 as an airborne tank, but this was not seriously pursued prior to its cancellation in 1958.

It was now understood that to field a vehicle light enough to be easily transported by air, some aspect of a tank's principal characteristics – armor, firepower, mobility – would have to be compromised. One possibility was to decrease or eliminate the armor protection and design a mobile gun to provide airborne units with mobile firepower. In the late 1940s, the airborne divisions were equipped with the widely despised 90mm M26 towed anti-tank gun, which was simply too clumsy to be a practical airborne weapon. In April 1949, the Army began a program to field a self-propelled 90mm gun as a more portable expedient than the inadequate towed anti-tank gun or some form of light tank.

Development was undertaken by the Cadillac Motor Car Division of General Motors and the first T101 pilots were completed in 1953 and tested by the Armor Board at Ft Knox in 1955. It was type-classified in 1958 as the M56 90mm self-propelled gun, though it was better known by its nickname as the Scorpion, or by its acronym SPAT (self-propelled anti-tank). It was built in very modest numbers, about 150 vehicles, with production ending in 1959. Besides being issued to airborne units, it was also used in the anti-tank companies of some infantry divisions in the late 1950s and early 1960s. The Scorpion was so light it could be airlifted by some of the heavy-lift helicopters of the day, and was also suitable for parachute dropping. Its main fault, aside from the obvious lack of armor, was the substantial recoil of its gun, which would lift the front of the vehicle into the air when firing. The Scorpion was adequate in a defensive anti-tank role, but its lack of armor made it unsuitable for providing offensive

A number of experimental weapons configurations were tried with the M56 SPAT at Ft Benning, such as the substitution of a 4.2in mortar, as seen here, or a 106mm recoilless rifle. (NARA)

The AAI Corporation's futuristic T92 was intended to replace the M41 light tank, but its lack of amphibious capability and doubts about its 76mm gun led to the more ambitious Sheridan program. (Author)

punch. With the advent of effective anti-tank missiles such as the new BGM-71 Tube-Launched, Optically Tracked, Wire-Guided (TOW) missile, the defensive role was better undertaken by missiles mounted on the M151 jeep. The Scorpion saw service in Vietnam with Company D, 16th Armor (Airborne Anti-Tank) of the 173rd Airborne Brigade, with these units having 17 vehicles each organized into three platoons. The lack of armor made it unsuitable for many missions and it was quickly retired. A total of 87 were provided to Morocco and five to Spain under the Military Aid Program (MAP).

In 1956, the Secretary of the Army authorized Project Whip to develop a new "Airborne Assault Weapon System." This was intended to be a vehicle with the firepower of a medium tank, but without the heavy armor. Although Project Whip did not progress into a specific weapon, the engineering studies conducted to support the program played a critical role in developing new anti-tank guided missile technologies that would feature in future airborne tank programs.

The initial batch of XM551 pilots used an unusual stamped road-wheel and a rigid swim-curtain contained in the aluminum hull. (NARA)

THE M551 SHERIDAN

Enter the Sheridan

The cancellation of the T92 light tank in 1958 was due in part to its lack of amphibious capability, a deficit that reduced its value in the cavalry reconnaissance role. In 1959, the US Army began work on a new Armored Reconnaissance Airborne Assault Vehicle (ARAAV) that was intended to fulfill the dual roles of an armored cavalry light tank and an airborne tank. The requirement stressed the need for amphibious features and air-drop capability, as well as substantially improved firepower over the 76mm gun that had been used on the M41 and T92 light tanks. Some 12 industrial proposals were offered, with a design concept from the Cadillac Motors Car Division of General Motors being selected for engineering development. The program began in June 1960 under the designation of XM551 ARAAV General Sheridan, named after the famous Civil War general, Phillip Sheridan. The centerpiece of the new tank was the 152mm XM81 Shillelagh Combat Vehicle Weapon System (CVWS).

Development of the CVWS was underway from April 1958 as a potential armament system for a variety of future tanks, including the joint US/German MBT-70. In contrast to conventional tank guns, the new CVWS was based around a guided missile that would be capable of penetrating at least 150mm of armor at 60 degrees. The missile requirement was predicated on the belief that a guided weapon could offer substantially better probability-of-hit than a conventional gun. Several designs were offered to satisfy this requirement, including the Polecat guided projectile from the Frankford Arsenal, and guided missile designs from Sperry and Ford-Aeronutronic. The Army issued a development contract to Ford-Aeronutronic in June 1959. The doubling of the weapon caliber from 76mm to 152mm Shillelagh was triggered both by the requirement for 150mm armor penetration and the size demands of contemporary guided-missile electronics. Given the state of shaped-charge warhead technology at the time, a very large warhead diameter was necessary. Although the centerpiece of the Shillelagh CVWS was the guided anti-tank missile, the weapon was also expected to fire more conventional unguided ammunition including high-explosive anti-tank (HEAT) and high-explosive/ fragmentation (HE-Frag) projectiles.

The Shillelagh missile used semi-automatic command line-of-sight (SACLOS) guidance based on an infrared command link. This type of guidance required the gunner to keep the sight on the target, and then the fire-control system automatically directed the missile to the target by tracking the missile's infrared flare, and sending course corrections via an infrared emitter. This was a second-generation development of anti-tank missile guidance; earlier command guidance systems actually required the gunner to steer the missile to its target using joystick controls. The second-generation SACLOS system offered a higher probability-of-hit and also demanded far lower levels of gunner training, since the guidance system did most of the work. The Shillelagh system presented a major engineering challenge due to the use of its infrared command link. A less ambitious SACLOS system was developed for the contemporary TOW anti-tank missile, which used a wire command link. Two of the major technical issues were the interference with the infrared command link caused by the missile exhaust plume and by ambient sunlight. The test launches began in November 1960 with the first guided test firings in September 1961.

The arrival of the new Kennedy administration in 1961, and most notably the new Secretary of Defense, Robert McNamara, accelerated the Shillelagh program. The Kennedy administration placed greater emphasis on US conventional forces, and McNamara's preference for technical solutions to tactical problems encouraged futuristic efforts such as Shillelagh. Since the XM551 Sheridan tank would take time to develop, McNamara supported an initial effort to deploy Shillelagh on the existing M60 tank as the M60A2. The first guided test launches of the Shillelagh missile in the autumn of 1961 at White Sands Missile Range (WSMR) were disappointing, with only one of 11 launches acceptable. The rocket motor smoke trail overwhelmed the infrared command link, so a new propellant was developed to minimize the smoke. The technological challenge posed by this futuristic weapon system

This is an M551 at Ft Knox in August 1967 from the early production series, evident from the turret fan cover on the rear left turret side instead of the eventual turret roof position, as well as the thick collar for the open breech scavenging system (OBSS) for the main gun. These early vehicles lack the smoke grenade launchers on the lower turret front. (NARA)

forced the Ordnance Tank Automotive Command (OTAC) to consider other armament options for the Sheridan and seven were considered, including 76mm, 90mm, 105mm, and 152mm guns, as well as a hybrid armament consisting of one of these guns supplemented by the existing French ENTAC wire-guided anti-tank missile, or a pure missile armament using either the TOW or Polecat missile. As the 76mm and 90mm guns offered little advance in firepower and as the TOW and Polecat were far from mature, OTAC decided to focus on the 152mm low-pressure gun being developed to launch the Shillelagh missile. This could still be used with conventional ammunition even if the missile proved unsuccessful, and it offered a major increase in firepower.

Firing tests of the modified missiles in May–June 1962 were far more satisfactory. The Shillelagh had one inherent weakness due to its infrared command link: it could not be effectively guided if the sun was directly behind the tank's command transmitter in roughly a 40-degree cone. The 1962 tests had been successful enough that Ford-Aeronutronic was awarded an extension of its development contract in January 1963 and consideration of alternative armament for the Sheridan faded. During the final development flight tests of the Shillelagh missile in September 1963 to October 1964, the missile performed satisfactorily in 58 of 63 launches; ten launches by military crews in September 1964 were successful. The MGM-51A Shillelagh missile was approved for limited production on August 12, 1964.

Due to the novelty of the 152mm gun/launcher, the focus of early Sheridan development was on the turret. A pilot turret was mounted on an M41 light tank hull and firing tests began at Aberdeen Proving Ground (APG) in August 1962 using the conventional 152mm ammunition. Twelve XM551 pilots were on order and the first were delivered in June 1962 for testing; the XM551 would go through five major production redesigns during the course of the pilot construction. Much of the redesign related to a folding swim barrier that provided the Sheridan with amphibious capabilities. The swim barrier was contained in a cavity around the upper edge of the hull and was designed to fold upward for river-crossing operations, and then fold down inside the hull when not in use. The first three pilots used a unique stamped aluminum road wheel and band track. This setup gave way to a more conventional concave road-wheel and link track on the fourth prototype and extensive redesign of the hull also took

On the standard production series, the turret ventilator was moved to the turret roof, as seen here. The M81E1 gun/launcher with closed breech scavenging system (CBSS) had a narrow tube without the thicker housing found on the initial M81 fitted with the earlier OBSS. This vehicle also has the forward portion of the "bird-cage" armor kit on the commander's .50-cal machine gun.

The Sheridan could swim water obstructions after erecting a flexible screen stowed in the upper edge of the hull. This is an early demonstration with E Troop, 19th Cavalry, 6th Infantry Division, near Schofield barracks in Hawaii in June 1968. (NARA)

place on this vehicle; three of this second batch of pilots were built in this configuration. The seventh pilot introduced yet the third redesign, shifting from a very substantial swim barrier on the front to a less obtrusive design, and adding a new swiveling driver's hatch. This third batch involved only a pair of vehicles, and with the arrival of the ninth pilot, the fourth batch began to resemble the eventual production configuration, eliminating the bulbous float covers on the road wheels and adding brushguards over the front headlights. The final pilot and fifth design introduced a modified flexible floatation barrier around the upper edge of the hull to provide the vehicle with a higher freeboard when in the water; this design would become the production configuration.

This is the gunner's station in the Sheridan, with the eyepiece for the M119 telescopic sight to the left and the XM44 passive night periscope to the right. (Author)

Funding for Sheridan production was included in the Fiscal Year 1966 (FY66) budget and a multi-year contract was awarded to General Motors' Allison Division on April 12, 1965, to manufacture it at the Cleveland Tank Automotive Plant. The Sheridan was approved as standard in May 1966, in spite of significant technical problems. The premature standardization was approved largely due to concern that to do otherwise would lead to the loss of funding in FY67 and the cancellation of the multi-year contract, effectively killing the program. As late as March 1966, the Army's Test and Evaluation Command (TECOM) at APG concluded that "as tested, it is not suitable for Army use because of specified safety, durability, reliability, performance, training, and maintenance limits." In June 1967, TECOM conducted tropical trials of the Sheridan in Panama and found that problems with the combustible case ammunition were so serious that Sheridan crews were prohibited from carrying more than a single round of ammunition in the vehicle at one time. This curtailed the

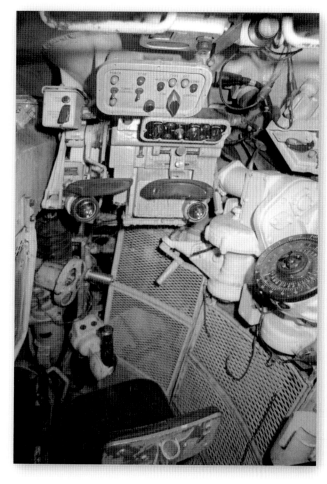

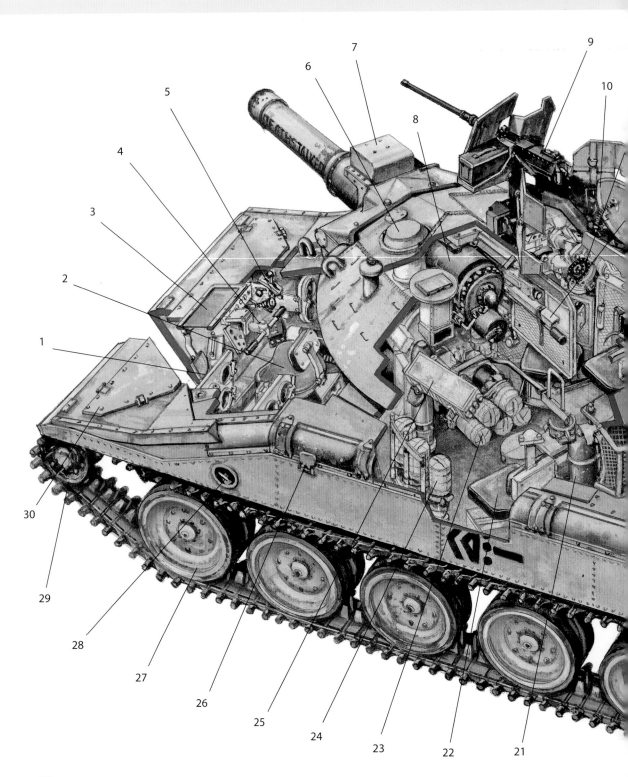

TECHNICAL DATA

Crew 4 (commander, gunner, loader, driver)

Length 6.27m (20.6ft)

Width 2.8m (9.2ft)

Height 2.9m (9.7ft)

Weight (combat loaded 15.2 tonnes (16.8 tons)

Road speed 71km/h (44mph)

Range 600km (375 miles)

Engine Detroit Diesel 6V53T 300hp diesel

Transmission Allison XTG-250-1A with multiple wet plate, mechanical brakes

Suspension Independent torsion bar

Main gun M81E1 152mm gun/launcher

Main gun ammunition 29 rounds (typically 10 missiles, 19 HEAT)

Missile armament Tube-launched, 152mm MGM-51 Shillelagh IR command-guided missile

Gunner's sights M127A1 telescope, AN/VSG-2 Tank Thermal Sight

Secondary armament Co-axial M240 7.62mm; .50-cal M2 heavy machine gun on pintle

Chemical protection Individual crew masks connected to central filter

Armor Frontal protection against .50-cal heavy machine gun

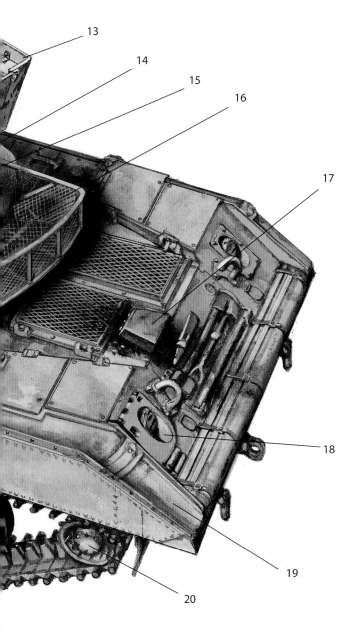

This view inside the Sheridan turret shows the breech to the right and the loader's station to the left. The M81E1 gun-launcher used a screw-breech for better sealing than the usual tank sliding breech-block. (Author)

The commander's station in the M551 featured a hand control that allowed the tank commander to swing the turret towards the target to cue the gunner and accelerate the firing sequence. (Author)

deployment of Sheridans beyond trials and training units until early 1968 and hundreds of newly manufactured Sheridans sat idle at depots.

The Sheridan's main problem at this point was indeed its combustible propellant case developed at Picatinny Arsenal. Unlike conventional ammunition that used a metal case, the Sheridan used a non-metallic case with a combustible nitrocellulose wall that contained the usual grained propellant inside. When the gun was fired, the propellant case and its contents were totally consumed. This radical approach had been taken largely because of its connection with the MBT-70 main battle tank (MBT) program which had an autoloader and nuclear/biological/chemical (NBC) protection system that required this feature.

The combustible case was much more fragile than metal cases and so there was a significant risk that it would break open and spill dangerous propellant grain on to the turret floor during the loading process. The case also tended to absorb moisture and would then swell, and so would not properly chamber in the gun. In addition, a damp case would sometimes not consume itself completely in the gun chamber when fired, so there was a risk that the

A test firing of the Shillelagh missile from a Sheridan at White Sands Missile Range in October 1967 shows the missile shortly after it has cleared the tube. (US Army)

subsequent round would come in contact with smoldering residue and prematurely detonate. Catastrophic premature detonations occurred three times during testing in November 1966 to March 1967 and the TECOM tests in Panama found that there was smoldering residue in the chamber in 39 percent of the firings. The original XM157 case was redesigned as the standard M157 and was issued in a neoprene bag to prevent the moisture problem; the bag was removed before the round was fired. The M205 third-generation casing entered development in May 1967, and was more rigid and less prone to breaking open. Although the Army considered the obvious solution of using a conventional metal case, this was rejected because the 152mm gun/launcher system was also being used on the new MBT-70 tank and metal-cased rounds were incompatible with its auto-loading system. In the event, the MBT-70 program was cancelled in 1971 and the Sheridan remained stuck with this immature technology.

The MGM-51 Shillelagh missile is seen here being loaded aboard one of the Sheridan pilots during early missile tests. (US Army)

The initial solution to the residue problem was use of an open breech scavenging system (OBSS) that blew carbon dioxide into the chamber. While the system was reasonably effective, it also blew smoldering residue back into the turret, which had the risk of coming into contact with the ammunition. In October 1967, the Army ordered Allison to halt the manufacture of the OBSS for the Sheridan. The continuing problems were so serious that there was another round of tests of alternative armament for the Sheridan, including the XM103E7 105mm howitzer and the 76mm gun; neither was adopted due to the subsequent developments. In late 1967, Allison developed a closed breech scavenging system (CBSS), which consisted of an air compressor and related equipment that blew the chamber clear after firing, but before the breech was opened. This system was approved for use in January 1968 starting with vehicle 700, but the initial 700 production vehicles remained in storage through much of 1969 until they could be retrofitted with the CBSS. The new system was designated as the M81E1, though it was often called the "152mm gun-launcher M81 modified."

An M551 "Two-Box" Sheridan of the 3/4th Cavalry in Vietnam during its initial combat deployment in December 1969. One of the first field modifications by the unit was to place an anti-RPG screen on the bow of the vehicle using chain link fence. (US Army)

Due to the space the CBSS took up, ammunition stowage was reduced from 30 rounds to 29. The original ammunition family for the Sheridan included the XM410 smoke, XM409 HEAT-T-MP (high-explosive anti-tank-tracer-multi-purpose), XM657E2 HE-Frag, and XM411 training round. The smoke and high-explosive rounds never entered production due to problems uncovered during tests, so the M409 round became the only conventional combat round aside from the Shillelagh missile. With deployment of the Sheridan to Vietnam, the M625 canister round was developed that contained 10,000 13-grain flechettes. When fitted with the improved M205 combustible case, the two upgraded rounds were re-designated as M409A1 and M625A1.

The first two M551 Sheridans were completed on July 29, 1966, and a total of 1,662 were delivered through November 2, 1970. The program cost was $1.3 billion, an 80 percent cost over-run compared to original estimates

D   **M551 SHERIDAN, 1/11TH "BLACKHORSE" ARMORED CAVALRY, BIEN HOA, VIETNAM, JANUARY 1969**

The markings of the 1/11th ACR were relatively simple, consisting of the registration number in white on the hull side and a stenciled maintenance marking on the lower rear hull regarding radio installation. The crew has chalked a vehicle name on the side. The 1/11th ACR used white bands on the gun tube to indicate the troops, in this case, three bands for Troop C.

M551 SHERIDAN, 3/4TH CAVALRY, 25TH DIVISION, CU CHI, VIETNAM, FEBRUARY 1969

The 3/4th Cavalry usually painted the red/white cavalry guidon on the hull side accompanied by a two-digit white tactical number. In this case, the tactical number is absent and the crew has painted a name in its place on the rear hull side. The 3/4th Cavalry painted a wide band around the gun tube indicating troops (A – red; B – white; C – blue).

D **M551 SHERIDAN, 1/11TH "BLACKHORSE" ARMORED CAVALRY, BIEN HOA, VIETNAM, JANUARY 1969**

M551 SHERIDAN, 3/4TH CAVALRY, 25TH DIVISION, CU CHI, VIETNAM, FEBRUARY 1969

Lingering concerns over the XM81 152mm gun/launcher led Rock Island Arsenal to test alternative armaments on the Sheridan chassis, including the 76mm gun used on the M41 light tank as seen here in March 1967. (US Army)

of $1.05 billion for for 2,426 Sheridans. A total of 88,194 Shillelagh missiles were manufactured by Ford-Aeronutronic and Martin at an average cost of $2,665 each. The Australian Army had considered the acquisition of the Sheridan and had tested a single vehicle in 1967–68, but rejected the design as "unsuitable for Vietnam-type conflicts – the only kind of war in which Australia is likely to be involved in the foreseeable future." The USMC considered the Sheridan for its Light Armored Combat Vehicle program to replace the Corps' M50 Ontos, but rejected it due to its cost and problems.

The Sheridan officially entered service use in June 1967 with 1/63rd Armor at Ft Riley, Kansas. To determine the effectiveness of the new Shillelagh missile, the unit was issued a relatively large number of the expensive missiles and in February 1968 fired 112 Shillelaghs, scoring 88 hits (78 percent). The first airborne deployment came shortly after with issue to the 1/17th Cavalry of the 82nd Airborne Division at Ft Bragg, and the first deployment outside the continental United States was the dispatch of ten Sheridans to the 19th Cavalry in Hawaii in April 1968. Authorization for overseas deployment came in October 1968, followed by authorization for the Eighth Army in South Korea in November 1968 and US Army Europe (USAREUR) in January 1969. By the autumn of 1971, there were about 800 Sheridans deployed, including 40 in South Korea, 310 in Europe, 250 in the United States and about 200 in Vietnam. In 1972, 64 Sheridans were issued for the first time to National Guard units in the US.

One of the technical problems to plague the Sheridan was the tendency of the missile system to signal a "no-go" when the checksight source lamp in the gunner's M149 telescopic sight was knocked out of alignment after firing the conventional ammunition. Although the developers blamed poor crew training and failure to perform alignment tests, the field commanders were not happy with a system that required such extensive maintenance. The slow pace of deployment and the continual complaints about vehicle reliability led to extensive criticism of the program by the US Congress and several Congressional investigations. One influential Congressman labeled the Sheridan "a billion-dollar boo-boo."

The Sheridan in Vietnam

The Sheridan had been designed as a high-tech counterweight to the overwhelming mass of Soviet tank forces in Central Europe through the use precise, long-range firepower. Instead, it would see its first combat deployment in the low-tech environment of Vietnam, minus its essential Shillelagh missile. In 1966, the Pentagon had first offered the Sheridan to the US Army in Vietnam, but at the time the main gun ammunition was unacceptable, and the tankers mocked it as a "$300,000 machine-gun platform." A US Army report on armored tactics in Vietnam in March 1967 foresaw the need for a light tank that had the mobility of the M113 APC, but with better firepower. While the M551 seemed the obvious solution, the report questioned the value of the Sheridan in Vietnam due to its lack of antipersonnel ammunition, lack of night-fighting capability, weak armor protection, and lack of a dozer kit. The report did not suggest that the Sheridan be modified for Vietnam, but in view of the controversy over the vehicle, OTAC saw this as an opportunity to redeem its controversial design. This led to a crash program to field the M625 flechette anti-personnel round, to develop an anti-mine belly armor package, and to improve the Sheridan's night-fighting capability. In 1968, after main gun ammunition was finally ready, a plan was approved to re-equip the 1st and 3rd Squadrons of the 4th Cavalry in Vietnam, but the unit was opposed to the plan due to the Sheridan's vulnerability to mines and anti-tank rockets compared to the M48A3 tank the unit was using.

The decision to deploy the Sheridan to Vietnam was largely the initiative of General Creighton Abrams, who had been appointed to command US forces in Vietnam in March 1968. Abrams had reluctantly approved type classification of the Sheridan while Army Vice Chief of Staff, and he was aggravated that 1,500 expensive vehicles were sitting unused at depots back in the United States. Abrams ordered the MACV J3 (Plans and Operations, Military Assistance Command, Vietnam) in Saigon to study the issue in July 1968. In view of the controversies swirling around the tank, Abrams wanted opinions from the users, not

An M551 "Two-Box" Sheridan in operation near Long Binh, Vietnam, on February 23, 1969, with B Troop, 1/11th Cavalry. This unit modified its Sheridans almost immediately with an extended bustle rack to accommodate the crew's gear. (NARA)

A common field modification of the M551 "Two-Box" Sheridans in Vietnam was the use of an armored shield over the commander's .50-cal machine gun, based on the pattern used on the M113 ACAV. This is a Sheridan of A Troop, 1/1st Cavalry of the Americal Division near Tam Ky on March 18, 1970. (US Army)

the developers. So the Ft Knox Armored School's Sheridan project officer, the Armor & Engineer Board M551 test officer, and the commander of the 73rd Tank Battalion where the M551 was in operational field test, were all brought to Saigon to brief Lieutenant-Colonel Burton Boudinot, heading the MACV J3 Sheridan project. After several days, the panel unanimously concluded that the M551 was not suitable for Vietnam in its current configuration. Abrams asked if the Sheridan would be of any use at all in Vietnam and Boudinot suggested that a limited deployment of the Sheridan would be instructive, but that only 27 vehicles should be sent, enough for a squadron, shorn of their Shillelagh missiles and complicated fire-control system, and reinforced with belly armor due to the mine threat in Vietnam.

The Sheridans modified for Vietnam were sometimes called the "Two-Box M551," as all the electronic boxes connected with the Shillelagh and fire control but for two were removed, the space used for additional machine-gun ammunition stowage, and the main ammunition racks configured only for conventional ammunition and not missiles. A total of 230 Sheridans were rebuilt or manufactured without the missile subsystem, vehicles 140–223 and 740–885. Abrams mentioned this debate to Colonel George S. Patton, commander of 11th Armored Cavalry, who suggested the best test would be

E

M551 SHERIDAN, 2ND ARMORED CAVALRY, US SEVENTH ARMY, GERMANY, 1974

During the 1970s, while the US Army in CONUS (Continental US) was being repainted with the new US Mobility Equipment Research and Development Center (MERDC) camouflage pattern, the US Seventh Army in Germany began to adopt its own expedient camouflage. The two predominant colors were FS 30277 Sand and FS 30117 Earth Red, with smaller areas of FS 34079 Forest Green and FS 37038 Black. The brown color varied more than the others and sometimes was mixed by the troops in depot, leading to erratic results. As part of the effort to camouflage their tactical vehicles, the usual white star gave way to a black star.

M551 SHERIDAN, 2ND ARMORED CAVALRY, US SEVENTH ARMY, GERMANY, 1974

to issue the Sheridan to a divisional squadron and a regimental squadron. So instead of 27 Sheridans, the Pentagon dispatched 64, enough for the use of two squadrons.

The first Sheridans arrived in Vietnam in January 1969 and were issued to the 3/4th Cavalry of the 25th Division and 11th Armored Cavalry Regiment (ACR). The 11th ACR had until then used a mixture of M113 APCs and M48A3 medium tanks, and were not keen on playing around with a lightly armored tank. Opinions changed a bit after the first combat encounter in the pre-dawn hours of January 29, 1969. Two Sheridans were on picket duty along the Long Binh highway when they spotted movement. After switching on the Sheridan's powerful searchlight, they engaged the enemy force with two rounds of the new M625 "bee-hive." The flechettes annihilated the enemy infantry formation and over 125 dead were found the next morning along with evidence that many walking-wounded had fled the scene. The M409 HEAT round was also found to be a devastating weapon used against houses and earthen bunkers. Since there was no official doctrine on the use of the Sheridan, both units created their own. The 11th ACR substituted three Sheridans for two M113 Armored Cavalry Vehicles (ACAVs) in one of three scout sections per armored cavalry platoon. While this arrangement decreased the number of dismounted scouts in the sections, it substantially increased their firepower. In reality, the units often deployed Sheridans from one section with several ACAVs from other sections to create a mixed force. The bee-hive round proved to be the most popular projectile in the Sheridan's arsenal; in the first three months of combat, the Sheridans fired 1,461 rounds of bee-hive compared to 350 rounds of M409 HEAT as well as 431,000 rounds of machine-gun ammunition.

The 3/4th Cavalry swapped Sheridans for M48A3 tanks in its platoons, a decision that proved far more controversial than the 11th ACR pattern. The old M48A3 was widely respected as a durable, reliable tank that was well suited to "jungle busting" due to its weight and horsepower. The 3/4th Cavalry lost its first Sheridan on February 15, 1969, when one ran over a mine, killing the driver, and leading to a catastrophic ammunition fire. The squadron "had its confidence shaken" according to a later Army report, as such mines were not so

A pair of M551s of E Troop, 17th Cavalry, 101st Airborne Division, at Ft Campbell in April 1972. These vehicles have the VSS-3 infrared searchlight, but lack the new bird-cage armor that was being introduced at this time. (NARA)

lethal against the much more substantial M48A3. Of the original 64 Sheridans, ten ran over mines within the first three months of operations, but only the first incident led to the total loss of the vehicle. The adoption of the special titanium anti-mine armor plates reduced the vulnerability of the Sheridan drivers to mines, though the mines often disabled the vehicle. After the three-month trial period, the Army in Vietnam was impressed enough with the Sheridan's performance that it would accept several hundred more tanks if certain deficiencies were addressed.

An M551 of Alpha Troop, 1/1st Cavalry, Americal Division, near Tam Ky, Vietnam, on March 18, 1970, shows the later features, including the formal bird-cage armor around the commander's cupola and the infrared searchlight. (NARA)

The main causes of Sheridan casualties in Vietnam were the ubiquitous RPG-2 and RPG-7 anti-tank rockets. In their first three months of deployment, 12 of the original 64 Sheridans were hit by RPGs, and five of the hits resulted in total losses. If the RPG penetrated near the turret, there was a very great risk that the combustible ammunition propellant would be hit, often leading to a chain reaction that set off a devastating ammunition fire. Such fires completely melted the aluminum armor of the Sheridan hull, leaving little more than a puddle of melted aluminum with the steel turret plopped in the debris. If the crew was inside the turret when this occurred, they had little hope of escaping. Many crews preferred to "ride shotgun" outside the turret rather than risk being trapped and incinerated inside the vehicle. The Sheridan turret was small and overcrowded because of all of the internal equipment and an Army report concluded that "the cramped fighting compartment and high turret temperatures did limit capabilities of the M551 crewmen… [tankers] became fatigued early, crew efficiency was affected, and the sustained firing rate reduced. During prolonged engagements, transfer of ammunition was slow and often hazardous."

The Sheridan was a maintenance burden in Vietnam, especially due to its complicated turret electronics. Some units grew so exasperated with the constant electrical malfunctions that they jerry-rigged a piece of communication wire between the gun's electrical firing mechanism and the turret dome light so that the main weapon could be fired if the usual methods were blocked by system failures. The humid conditions led to ammunition

An M551 Sheridan of E Troop, 2nd Armored Cavalry, in Germany in 1974, one of two armored cavalry regiments that relied on the Sheridan through the 1970s. It is fitted with the new bird-cage armor and VVS-3 searchlight, but has yet to be fitted with the laser rangefinder. (Russ Vaughan)

problems due to the swelling of the combustible cartridge, and in the three-month trial in 1969, 41 misfires occurred. These posed a real dilemma to the crew in combat, since the only way to extract the round was to ram it out from the muzzle end. Several crews suffered casualties while doing this while in contact with the enemy. The ammunition was vulnerable to damage from mine shock and vibration, and 140 rounds were damaged during the trials, with the projectile splitting off from the cartridge case. The engine proved to be a frequent source of problems due to overheating, in part due to faulty fanbelts as well as the propensity of the radiator and air filters to become clogged in jungle and dusty conditions. Twenty-five engines of the original 64 had to be replaced during the three-month trials.

A common improvisation in Vietnam was to relocate the commander's turret control handle to permit the tank commander to traverse and fire the main gun while sitting outside the turret on top of the commander's cupola. Often, the main gun would be pre-loaded with a bee-hive round, which did not require precision aiming to be effective against enemy infantry. The ammunition can feeding the 7.62mm co-axial machine gun in the turret was also a source of frustration due to its inadequate amount of ammunition and the tendency to jam. These were quickly replaced by larger cans taken from M48A3 tanks, or spare 20mm ammunition cans from helicopter mini-guns.

The combat and climate conditions in Vietnam required many other modifications to the Sheridan. One of the earliest upgrades was to mount the .50-cal armored shield from M113 ACAVs on the commander's .50-cal machine gun. This eventually led to the development of an "armored bird-cage" to offer the Sheridan commander better protection against small-arms fire. While operating in the heavy bush of Vietnam, the Sheridan exhaust fumes could be trapped near the vehicle by the dense foliage, and many crews improvised an exhaust extension from metal artillery transport tubes to conduct the exhaust further away from the turret. Another common modification was the addition of stowage bins on the rear of the turret to compensate for the small stowage rack provided on the baseline vehicle.

In spite of the numerous difficulties with the Sheridan, it eventually proved to be a useful addition to the armored cavalry when used as a substitute for the M113 ACAV, but not as a substitute for the more robust M48A3 tank. The Sheridan's main advantage was that it was more mobile on soft terrain than the heavier M48A3. As a result, additional Sheridans were shipped to Vietnam for use by other armored cavalry units so that by 1970, about 200 were in service. In total, some 300 Sheridans were damaged or knocked out in combat, of which about 90 were total write-offs. The Sheridan was never popular in Vietnam, however, even if it did prove to be a superior source of firepower to the M113 ACAV. Its vulnerability to enemy fire and lingering mechanical and electrical unreliability left it with a reputation as troublesome and dangerous.

The Electric War-Machine

While the Sheridan was being combat-tested in Vietnam, it was also being issued to armored cavalry units in the United States, USAREUR, and elsewhere, often accompanied by civilian technicians to help iron out lingering technical deficiencies. Sheridan strength in USAREUR went from 309 in late 1971 to 576 at the completion of the deployment program in 1974, equipping 32 troop units.

The M551 proved to be difficult vehicle to tame due to the complexity of the electronic systems in the turret, leading some soldiers to dub it "the Electric War-Machine." The firepower of the Sheridan was fearsome, and the tank leapt up off its first two or three road-wheels when the M409 HEAT round was fired. Gunners were instructed to keep their faces firmly pressed against the sight when firing to avoid injury, and the standard recognition feature of Sheridan gunners was a perennial black eye. The Sheridan suspension lacked return rollers and at slow road speeds this setup produced harmonic vibrations that loosened parts. When subjected to the violence of the recoil when firing the M409 HEAT round, bits of the tanks would occasionally come off, including the searchlight, birdcage armor, and various

The "60th Motor Rifle Regiment" of the "Krasnovian Army" formed the core of the opposing forces (OPFOR) at the US Army's new National Training Center at Ft Irwin, California, in the 1980s. It was equipped with 330 M551A2 OPFOR VISMODs in various configurations, including a surrogate for the Soviet T-80 main battle tank as seen here. These were armed solely with laser simulators. (Author)

internal components. Shillelagh missiles were seldom fired in peacetime due to their high cost and were usually reserved for special occasions such as exercises at the Grafenwohr firing ranges.

There were a number of attempts to improve the Shillelagh and the M81 gun/launcher. The MGM-51B extended-range Shillelagh was developed, which increased the maximum range from 2,000 to 3,000m. During initial service, the gun tube was found to have a service life of only 100 rounds due to structural cracks at the muzzle end. Although the M81 used a smooth-bore gun tube, it had a shallow groove that fitted a "key" on the missile that kept the missile in a fixed vertical orientation prior to launch to establish its proper flight regime. By the time the M81 entered service in 1967, the service life of the barrel was raised to 200 rounds by various manufacturing improvements, though the goal was 500 rounds. The eventual solution was to reduce the dimension of the key on the missile, and the "shallow-key" Shillelagh was standardized in January 1968 as the MGM-51C and became the most common version of the missile.

The advent of the Sheridan with its substantial firepower raised the issue of the role of the armored cavalry regiments in Germany. Through the 1970s, their doctrine was debated, with USAREUR leaning towards their use as a potent anti-armor force. This issue was never formally settled, in no small measure due to the short life of the Sheridan in USAREUR.

The Sheridan underwent a series of improvements in the early 1970s to rectify problems and add capabilities. In light of the Vietnam experience, the addition of bird-cage armor around the commander's cupola became standard, even in USAREUR. The co-axial .30-cal machine gun was a source of problems and the original M73 gave way to the improved M71E1, the M219, and finally the M240 machine gun in the late 1970s. The initial production version of the Sheridan lacked an infrared searchlight, relying only on its XM44 image intensification sight. Since this was inadequate on moonless or cloudy nights, the German AEG XS30U searchlight as used on the Leopard 1 tank was added, starting with vehicle 140. This fitting was short-lived, and most Sheridans received the AN/VSS-3 searchlight.

One of the most significant improvements in the Sheridan was the adoption of an AN/VVG-1 laser rangefinder, the first installed on a US tank.

The M551A1 was the first US tank equipped with a laser rangefinder to improve gun accuracy. The rangefinder was added on to the commander's cupola below the machine-gun tripod, as seen on this example of the 2nd ACR in Germany in 1974. (Russ Vaughan)

The Sheridan had a more urgent requirement for this system than tanks with conventional guns, as its standard M409 projectile was unusually slow and had a pronounced ballistic arc, mandating greater elevation correction than typical high-velocity ammunition. The laser rangefinder was packaged in a small unit placed immediately in front of the commander's cupola and under the .50-cal machine-gun mount. The electronics for the unit were packaged in boxes placed in the rear of the armored bird-cage. The laser was not integrated into the gunner's fire-controls; the commander lased the target and gave the range information to the gunner via the intercom. The gunner's telescopic sight was modified into the M127A1 configuration, which had a laser filter to prevent eye damage; the VVG-1 was not eye-safe. Approval for the production of 505 VVG-1s came on April 22, 1971, with deliveries beginning in 1972.

The Sheridan was never an especially popular vehicle in the US Army in spite of its firepower. The string of improvements never entirely cured its many reliability faults. Although it was automotively dependable, the massive recoil of its gun/launcher was not compatible with the Shillelagh missile. The Sheridan had an operational ready rate of only 66 percent in June 1974, over five years after initial deployment, and it did not reach the goal of 80 percent until June 1975 after an extensive improvement and training program. By the time it exceeded the USAREUR standard of 88 percent in 1977, its fate was already in doubt. The Army was already planning a new generation of ACAV, first the XM800 Armored Reconnaissance Scout Vehicle (ARSV), and subsequently the M3 Bradley Cavalry Fighting Vehicle, and so there was some debate regarding the fate of the Sheridan. In the summer of 1977, there was a meeting of the Army Chief of Staff, General Edward "Shy" Meyer, with Training and Doctrine

Another of the M551A2 VISMODs replicated the Soviet ZSU-23-4 Shilka, as seen here in the Mojave desert in 1990. (Author)

Although first deployed to Saudi Arabia with the M551A1 in 1990, the 3/73rd Armor was re-equipped with the upgraded M551A1(TTS) as quickly as they were remanufactured at the Anniston depot. (US DoD)

Command (TRADOC) commander General Donn Starry, and Army Material Command (AMC) commander General John Guthrie. Starry had commanded the 11th ACR in 1970 in Vietnam after it had transitioned to the Sheridan, and he repeated the litany of woes of the Sheridan, recommending its retirement along with the equally troubled M60A2 tank, also armed with the Shillelagh. Although Guthrie tried to defend the Sheridan, Starry was far

F   M551 SHERIDAN, 1ST CAVALRY, FT HOOD, TEXAS, 1974

After over a half-century of plain olive drab finishes, in the early 1970s the US Army began to camouflage-paint its combat vehicles. In 1972, MERDC at Ft Belvoir began experimenting with a variety of camouflage patterns and paints, finally settling on a four-color system in 1973. The patterns were designed to be suitable for eight environments: Europe/US winter verdant; snow temperate forested; snow temperate open terrain, Europe/US summer verdant, verdant tropics; gray desert; red desert; arctic winter. The system was designed to minimize the need for repainting. So for example, vehicles painted in the winter verdant scheme as seen here, could be switched to the summer verdant scheme simply by re-painting the field drab portions with light green. The patterns relied on 12 camouflage colors that were essentially the same as had been used by the US Army engineers since World War II. The two principal colors covered about 45 percent each of the surface, while the two subsidiary colors covered only about 5 percent each and were mainly intended to break up the pattern. The system's most distinctive designs were the black "crows' feet" patterns. At the same time, the US Army switched from olive drab to forest green as its standard tactical camouflage color, and all new equipment purchased was delivered from the manufacturer in this color. The first unit finished in these colors was a brigade of the 2nd Armored Division at Ft Hood in the summer of 1973, followed by the 1st Cavalry. The winter verdant scheme was actually one of the most popular schemes in the southwestern US, as the field drab color tended to blend with the dried prairie grass. The scheme consisted of FS 34079 Forest Green and FS 30118 Field Drab as the predominant colors and FS 30277 Sand and FS 37038 Black as the subsidiary colors.

M551A1 SHERIDAN, CO. C, 3/73RD ARMOR, OPERATION *JUST CAUSE*, PANAMA, DECEMBER 1989

In 1983, the US Army agreed to adopt the new NATO three-color camouflage scheme of FS 30051 Green, FS 34094 Brown, and FS 37030 Black based on the German Bundeswehr system. The M551A1 Sheridans of the 3/73rd Armor were repainted in this new scheme. The battalion had adopted its own scheme of tactical markings based on a forward-pointing chevron to indicate the company, in this case three chevrons for Co. C, and three dots behind this indicating the 3rd Platoon.

F M551 SHERIDAN, 1ST CAVALRY, FT HOOD, TEXAS, 1974

M551A1 SHERIDAN, CO. C, 3/73RD ARMOR, OPERATION *JUST CAUSE*, PANAMA, DECEMBER 1989

All packed up and ready to go! The 3/73rd Armor kept a number of its M551A1(TTS) Sheridans pre-packaged with their parachutes and airborne pallets at Ft Bragg as part of a ready-brigade, able to be inserted rapidly by air around the globe. (Author)

more eloquent in his condemnation of the design, and Meyer agreed to retire it with all deliberate speed. Since the M3 Bradley was not yet ready, the short-term solution was simply to dump the Sheridan in favor of the existing M60A1 MBT. At the time, there were 867 in USAREUR, 535 in the continental US, and 41 in the Pacific in Hawaii and South Korea. The conversion of the armored cavalry units in USAREUR began in June 1978 and was completed in April 1979 and in the rest of the Army by 1980. The exception to the retirement plan was a single armor battalion with the 82nd Airborne Division, and a dozen vehicles in service with the National Guard. The "residual fleet" was drawn down to 140 vehicles, the remainder being held in pre-positioned reserve.

AIRBORNE OPERATIONS

The 82nd Airborne Division was the only unit to regularly make use of the M551 Sheridan in the airborne role. When first deployed with the 82nd Airborne Division in 1967 for operational trials, the vehicles were attached to 1/17th Cavalry, 3rd Brigade. The 1/17th Cavalry was later transferred to the 101st Airmobile Division and the 82nd Airborne Division was allotted the 4/68th Armor, which was re-flagged in February 1984 as the 3/73rd Armor.

Three methods were available for air-delivery of the Sheridan: air-landing from a transport aircraft, parachute drop, or low-altitude drop. With the advent of large transports with ramps such as the C-130 Hercules and C-141 Starlifter, the Sheridan could be delivered if there was a suitable airfield. For forced entry, the other two methods were needed. Parachute drop could be undertaken using the C-130 or C-141 using low-velocity air drop (LVAD) techniques. The Sheridan was packaged on a special pallet with layers of crushable honeycomb aluminum sheet below, and eight G-11A cargo parachutes. A far more dramatic method was the low-altitude parachute extraction system (LAPES). As in the case of more conventional parachute delivery, the Sheridan was mounted on a special pallet with crushable honeycomb below to help cushion the impact. The Sheridan would be carried into the drop area by C-130 Hercules transport aircraft, which would fly as low and as slow as possible over the landing area. A set of extraction parachutes would drag the Sheridan on its pallet out of the aircraft, and it would fall five to ten feet to the ground at speeds of under a hundred miles per hour, skidding across the ground for hundreds of feet before finally coming to a halt. This method offered some spectacular opportunities for mishaps, and on more than one occasion, a Sheridan ended up somersaulting all over the landing zone.

The US Army Tank and Automotive Command (TACOM) started a Sheridan mid-life product improvement program (PIP) in 1974, and vehicles were modified in 1977–80 with 26 automotive changes, including the replacement of the original 6V53T aluminum block engine with a cast-iron block version. Following the retirement of the Sheridan by most of the Army, the 3/73rd Armor at Ft Bragg continued to sponsor some modest upgrades. The troublesome M176 smoke mortars were replaced by a new-generation smoke grenade system developed for the M2/M3 Bradley fighting vehicle. The M219 7.62mm co-axial machine gun was, as already noted, replaced by the M240, the fourth and final change to this perennially troublesome weapon. In 1989, TACOM initiated a program to improve the Sheridan's night vision systems. The gunner's fire controls were reconfigured by the substitution of the AN/VSG-2 Tank Thermal Sight (TTS) from the M60A3 tank, while the driver was provided with a second-generation image-intensification night sight derived from the system used on the new M2/M3 Bradley. The upgrade was undertaken at the Anniston Army Depot where most of the retired Sheridan fleet was stored, and this version was designated as M551A1(TTS). The plan was to complete the upgrade of 70 vehicles by April 1991, but the Iraqi invasion of Kuwait in August 1990 abruptly accelerated the program, as the 82nd Airborne Division was slated for immediate deployment to Saudi Arabia. As a result, the program was completed in only 45 days, with 60 of the Sheridans sent to Saudi Arabia, and the rest remaining in the United States for training.

The US Marine Corps LAV-25 was considered as a supplement or substitute for the Sheridan in the late 1980s and a single scout platoon was deployed with the 3/73rd Armor from 1986 through the Gulf War. (Author)

The Navy Surface Weapons Center adapted the standard NATO 105mm gun to the Sheridan as a contender for the Marine Corps' Mobile Protected Weapon System (MPWS) requirement in 1983. (US DoD)

There were so many Sheridans sitting idle at Anniston depot that 3/73rd Armor considered the idea of developing a paratroop fighting vehicle based on a turretless Sheridan. This was intended as an airborne equivalent of the Bradley Infantry/Cavalry Fighting Vehicle or the Soviet BMD airborne vehicle. Several prototypes were locally constructed at Ft Bragg and armed with a 25mm Bushmaster cannon or a TOW anti-tank missile launcher. Although used on an experimental basis in the mid-1980s, these modifications were never formally accepted by the Army. A Soviet-style mechanized airborne force has never been considered seriously by the US Army due to doubts that enough air transport would be available.

The most extensive use of the Sheridan after the 1979 retirement was the allocation of 330 vehicles to the Army's National Training Center at Ft Irwin in California's Mojave desert. These were rebuilt as Visual Modifications (VISMODs) to simulate standard Soviet AFVs such as the T-80, BMP, 2S1, and ZSU-23-4, and were officially designated as M551A2 Opposing Force Vehicle. They were deployed with the "60th Guards Motor Rifle Division of the Krasnovian Army," the principal opposing force unit for force-on-force wargames and training. The vehicles were armed only with laser simulators and blank-firing devices. These were the longest-serving Sheridans in the US Army, and were retired in 2004.

Airborne Sheridans in Combat

The first operational use of the Sheridan since Vietnam was during Operation *Just Cause* in Panama in December 1989, the only combat parachute drop of tanks in history. The political crisis was long in brewing, and a platoon of

M551A1(TTS), CO. D, 3/73RD ARMOR, 82ND AIRBORNE DIVISION, IRAQ, OPERATION DESERT STORM, FEBRUARY 1991
In the early 1980s, the US Army Mobility Equipment Research And Development Command (MERADCOM; formerly MERDC) was developing a new paint formulation called CARC (chemical agent resistant coating), which was a polyurethane paint that did not dissolve like previous enamels and lacquers when washed with chemical decontamination solutions. As a result, when the US Army went over to the new NATO camouflage patterns in 1985, it also adopted the new CARC paint. Besides the three NATO colors, paint was also developed for other environments, notably desert environments. So when US forces deployed to Kuwait in 1990, CARC Tan 686, which is equivalent to FS 33446 Tan, was applied to tactical vehicles.

One of the options was to re-arm the Sheridan, and Pacific Car and Foundry offered this alternative with the ELKE mount with the Ares 75mm automatic cannon. (PCFDI)

four M551A1 Sheridan tanks from 3/73rd Armor was flown into Panama in November 1989 and left hidden in a hanger at Howard Air Force Base, with their troops in mufti wearing 5th Infantry Division patches, since that formation regularly conducted jungle training in Panama. Sheridan support was deemed vital, as the Panamanian Defense Forces (PDF) operated a number of light armored vehicles.

Operation *Just Cause* was intended to overthrow the regime of Manuel Noriega by the surprise use of overwhelming force to minimize damage and bloodshed. A reaction brigade of the 82nd Airborne Division was inserted by parachute at Tocumen airport in the pre-dawn darkness of December 20, 1989, and included ten Sheridans of Co. C, 3/73rd Armor, which were parachuted from C-141B transports rather than air-landed. Two of these came to grief after landing in a marsh covered with elephant grass, with one being destroyed when its parachutes failed to deploy and another damaged; the tankers parachuted separately from the tanks. The Sheridans helped to lead paratrooper columns to their objectives, blasting Panamanian roadblocks with their massive 152mm rounds. The Sheridans already in Panama were moved to Quarry Heights near the PDF's "La Comandancia" headquarters and took part in the final fighting to overcome the opposing forces. Major Frank Sherman, who led the Sheridans in Panama, concluded that "the M551A1 Sheridans of the Army's parachute tank battalion continue to offer the commander the decisive edge." The after-action report noted: "The presence of Sheridans raised the morale of friendly forces and Panamanian civilians. They had an extreme psychological effect on enemy forces and looters. Once Sheridans moved into an area or after an initial engagement involving the M551A1s, enemy forces generally refused to fire or snipe at convoys or positions in the vicinity of the Sheridans."

With the Sheridans increasingly showing their age by the mid-1980s, the Army began to examine whether the Marine Corps' wheeled General Motors LAV-25 (Light Armored Vehicle – 25mm gun) might be suitable as a

substitute or alternative for airborne support. Given the Army designation M1047, 14 of these were tested at Ft Bragg from 1987, including parachute and LAPES delivery tests. Although very useful as scout vehicles, they did not have enough firepower to replace the Sheridan and they were a bit top-heavy for LAPES.

AAI Corporation developed this futuristic light tank armed with an Ares 75mm automatic cannon for the HSTV-L effort. (AAI Corp)

Following the Iraqi invasion of Kuwait in August 1990, the 3/73rd Armor again saw combat deployment, this time to Saudi Arabia for Operation *Desert Shield*. In this case, the 82nd Airborne Division was air-landed to provide an immediate barrier force against any possible incursion by the Iraqi Army. The air-landed Sheridans were the only US tanks in Saudi Arabia until further forces could be moved by sea. The 3/73rd Armor was initially equipped with its existing M551A1 tanks, but as the upgraded M551A1 (TTS) tanks were completed at the Anniston depot they were shipped to Saudi Arabia. Eleven M1047 LAVs were deployed as a scout platoon of 3/73rd Armor. As part of the subsequent assault into Iraq as part of Operation *Desert Storm*, the 3/73rd Armor saw its first tank-vs-tank fighting. The 82nd Airborne Division was used as a flanking force in the Iraqi desert, and overran the remnants of the Iraqi 45th Division. At least one Shillelagh was used against an Iraqi T-55 or Type 59, the only time this missile was fired in anger. The Sheridans performed extremely well and there were no mechanical breakdowns.

The US Army announced that it would disband the 3/73rd Armor on September 11, 1996, with the inactivation occurring over the following year. Although the M551A2 VISMOD Sheridans continued to serve at NTC until 2004, this marked an end to the combat career of the M551 Sheridan. For contingency operations, an Immediate Ready Company (IRC) from the 3rd Infantry Division at Ft Stewart, Georgia, equipped with M1A1 Abrams tanks and Bradley fighting vehicles, was assigned to augment the 82nd Airborne Division when armored support was needed, with plans to airlift them to combat using the new C-17 transport aircraft.

Teledyne Continental proposed its TCM-20 chassis with an overhead 105mm low-pressure gun for the Armored Gun System (AGS). (Teledyne Continental)

THE ELUSIVE QUEST FOR PERFECTION

The hasty retirement of most Sheridans in 1978 left the US Army in a quandary about the need for a future light tank and whether the approach should be an evolution of the existing M551 Sheridan or an entirely new design. The general consensus in the early 1980s was that the Sheridan's main problem was its flawed 152mm gun/launcher, but that the basic chassis was sound. As a result, there were a variety of schemes to modify the large pool of existing Sheridan hulls with various armament options. In parallel, the Army was also exploring a new generation of vehicles to satisfy its need for a tank that would be suitable for rapid deployment in contingency operations.

The Defense Advanced Research Programs Agency (DARPA) sponsored a variety of study programs to examine different advanced armored vehicle technologies under its High Mobility/Agility (HIMAG) vehicle program starting in 1976, which later became part of an Army TACOM effort. The Army program eventually spawned light tank design efforts such as the High Survivability Test Vehicle – Light (HSTV-L), which led to the construction of a number of prototypes armed with a rapid-fire 75mm gun. One of the spin-offs from this program was the Elevated Kinetic Energy (ELKE) gun system that was mounted on a surplus Sheridan hull for trials purposes in 1982. None of these programs progressed beyond testing, as the 75mm gun had insufficient lethality against Soviet tanks while at the same time not having adequate high-explosive firepower for use against other targets.

The Iranian embassy hostage crisis of the late 1970s prompted both the US Army and USMC to consider their future armored vehicle requirements for a Rapid Deployment Force (RDF) that was specifically configured for rapid insertion into hotspots around the globe, combining both armored firepower and a light logistical footprint. This deployment brief implied a light tank, and the Marine requirement was dubbed the Mobile Protected Weapon System (MPWS). The Marines considered adapting the existing

105mm tank gun to the surplus Sheridan fleet, and a Sheridan was rebuilt by the Naval Surface Weapons Center Laboratory in Dahlgren, Virginia, in 1983 to test the concept; the program never received enough support to reach the production stage. The Army initially planned a Mobile Protected Gun (MPG) program that would be fielded by the experimental 9th Infantry Division (Motorized). In December 1984, the Army announced plans to ship 41 Sheridan tanks to the 9th Division and eventually modify a further 120 Sheridans with 105mm or 120mm guns. This program was very short-lived and was cancelled in April 1985 after a study concluded that the Army lacked sufficient spare parts and that the cost would be too high to win Congressional support.

After this setback, the Army restarted the light tank project under yet another name, XM4 Armored Gun System (AGS). Private industry proposed vehicles for this requirement, including the AAI RDF Light Tank, Cadillac-Gage's Stingray export tank, Teledyne-Continental's TCM-20 AGS, and FMC Corp's Close Combat Vehicle – Light (CCVL). The program suffered from roller-coaster funding and Congressional interference. The requirement for air-drop capability was eliminated in March 1991, and Congress tried to force the Army to buy the Marine Corps' wheeled LAV-105. This effort ended abruptly when the Marines cancelled the LAV-105. Other potential contenders included the Swedish Hägglunds IKV-91 tank destroyer, re-armed with a 105mm gun. In the event, the Army finally settled on the FMC Corp CCVL as the basis for the newly re-designated XM8 AGS.

The XM8 represented a response to the technological lessons of the Sheridan, favoring existing automotive and firepower technology rather than futuristic approaches. With the Cold War now over, the focus shifted from confrontations with the tank-heavy forces of the Warsaw Pact to contingency

Cadillac Gage developed its Stingray with a low-recoil 105mm gun as an export tank, and sold over a hundred to Thailand. Alternatives included a separate vehicle, as well as one with the turret mounted on the Sheridan hull. (Cadillac Gage)

operations more similar to Panama or Operation *Desert Shield*. The chassis used components derived from the M2/M3 Bradley and the vehicle was armed with a derivative of the standard NATO 105mm gun, the low-recoil XM35 gun. To minimize weight and size, the AGS used a two-man turret crew and autoloader. In its basic "level 1" configuration, the design was intended to provide armor against heavy machine-gun fire; level 2 and level 3 added progressively greater levels of appliqué armor to offer better protection against common battlefield threats, such as the ubiquitous RPG. The idea behind this was that the AGS could be deployed by air in its light, level 1 configuration, and the appliqué armor shipped separately if needed and mounted in theater; the vehicle weighed between 19 and 25 tons in combat-loaded configuration depending on the armor package. This provided the Army with a more versatile vehicle that could have heavier armor when needed, and greater portability for scenarios where the anti-armor threat was not as great.

Six XM8 pilots were delivered in April–May 1994, with the Army objective at the time to acquire 237 AGS vehicles to equip the 3/73rd Armor and the 2nd ACR. Although the program proceeded very quickly due to the maturity of the design, the Army was in considerable turmoil on account of budget and force cuts in the wake of the end of the Cold War. In 1995, the Army considered dropping the plans to equip the 2nd ACR with the AGS. In spite of this, the Army approved the production of the AGS on October 27, 1995, as the M8 with a first contract for 26 vehicles. However, on January 24, 1996, the Army finally decided to kill the AGS program for cost-cutting reasons, largely based on the decision against deploying it with the 2nd ACR; it was unaffordable if built only for a single battalion of the 82nd Airborne Division.

In March 2004, the Army approved the transfer of four of the M8 AGS in storage to Ft Bragg for further examination of airborne armor requirements. The army has a number of light armored gun programs underway, including the M1128 Mobile Gun System (MGS), a member of the Stryker family of wheeled armored vehicles. The Strykers are not intended for air-drop, though they can be used in rapid-deployment scenarios. The Army's Future Combat Systems (FCS) is also exploring a variety of light armored vehicles, but the program has faltered in recent years and may be at risk of cancellation or restructuring. In recent decades, airborne tanks have been viewed by the US Army as too specialized to justify the cost.

FURTHER READING

The history of the M22 Locust has been obscure, though the recent book by Keith Flint provides a thorough examination of British use; I used the official M22 development history from the Ordnance files at the National Archives and Records Administration (NARA) in College Park, Maryland, for this account. The Sheridan has been well covered over the years, notably in the superb book by Richard Hunnicutt. The House Armed Services Committee report is particularly instructive about the many controversies surrounding the Sheridan's development program.

Government Reports and Documents
Review of the Army Tank Program (Report of the House Armed Services Committee, July 9, 1969)
M551 Sheridan Weapon System Handbook (Department of the Army, nd)
M551/M551A1 Instructor's Handbook (Armor School, June 1976)
Operator's Manual (Turret Operation) AR/AAV M551 Sheridan: TM 9-2350-230-10/2-1 (Department of the Army, March 31, 1973)
Operator's Manual AR/AAV M551A1, M551 NTC: TM 9-2350-230-10 (Department of the Army, May 11, 1992)
DeLong, E. et al., *History of the Shillelagh Missile System 1958–1982* (US Army Missile Command, 1984)
Starry, General Donn, *Mounted Combat in Vietnam* (Department of the Army, 1978)

Books
Flint, Keith, *Airborne Armour* (Helion, 2004)
Hunnicutt, Richard, *Sheridan: A History of the American Light Tank* (Presidio, 1995)
Mesko, Jim, *M551 Sheridan in Action* (Squadron, 1990)

Articles
Boudinot, Lieutenant Colonel Burton, "A Sheridan Memoir: The Early Days," *Armor* (January–February 1997) pp.14–15
deClaire, Robert, "M551 Material Product Improvement Program," *Army R&D News Magazine* (August–September 1977, pp.12–13)
Duffy, Michael, "9th Division Gets New Dune Buggy but an Old Tank," *Defense Week* (January 21, 1985) p.1
McElhaney, Becky, and Joan Gustafson, "Patriotism in Action," *Ordnance* (August 1991) pp.8–11
McKaughan, Jeff, "Operation Just Cause," *Journal of Military Ordnance* (July 1999) pp.25–27
Sherman, Major Frank, "Operation Just Cause: The Armor-Infantry Team in the Close Fight," *Armor* (September–October 1996) pp.34–35
Varljen, Colonel Frank, "More Sheridan Memoirs," *Armor* (May– June 1997) pp.38–39

INDEX

Figures in **bold** refer to illustrations.